LOIS AND MEL

THE BEGINNING

SASQUATCH SENIOR COMMUNITY
BOOK 2

PATRICK TALMADGE

HANGAR 1 PUBLISHING

1

TRAVELING TO ORMOND BEACH FLORIDA

The year was 1955, when Lois and Mel were still working for the FBI. They ran an insurance business as a front, so they could travel the country and world checking on the newest inventions, without suspicion of their real intentions or identities. Mel was a mechanical engineering genius, and Lois was an expert in the new field of computer electronics. The FBI used them to look at and determine the real value to American defense of new inventions without anyone or any country being aware. Mel and Lois would visit the inventors under the umbrella of insurance agents investigating to insure the inventions. That way, they could secretly examine the inventions and not draw attention to the inventors in the event the invention was critical for national defense.

Mel and Lois had traveled by train to Florida without much information on the invention they were going to examine. It turned out a group of car racing enthusiasts in Ormond Beach had built a unique flying craft and planned to show it off to the press next week. The garage had not given much information to the press, but something about how it floated first drew the FBI's attention. The FBI determined it may be of great importance and wanted them to check it out before the world saw it. They knew it involved flying and electronics, but Mel and Lois had no other information before they saw the craft.

Last week, Lois had called the owner of the Ormond Garage to set up an appointment to discuss getting upgraded insurance. Due to their racing success, the value of their race cars and equipment in the garage increased, plus she told them, businesses nearby were worried about possible fire problems because of the stored fuel the cars used. There were no actual worries from neighboring businesses, but it was a way to get inside and see the flying craft before the major press announcement. If the flying craft was as big a deal as their presence suggests, then Mel and Lois would need to stop the press announcement, and the FBI would confiscate the craft. Mel hated the idea of taking a man's invention, but it was needed if national security or defense was at stake.

Once Mel and Lois arrived at the train station, a car was waiting for them. Mel opened the trunk to make sure the car contained all their test equipment, including some of the Bureau's newest scientific equipment and fun gadgets. A quick survey showed all his needed equipment was there and what looked like Lois's fancy electronic gadgets. Mel read the label on one small box and was going to have to ask Lois what TV glasses were. He began smiling, thinking about glasses with the small TV's you watched.

Lois yelled to Mel from the front seat, saying, "the stuff will still be there when we get to the garage, so get a move on before it gets dark."

Mel sighed and said, "OH, now Lois," then he got in and drove to the Ormond Garage, or as the locals call it, Gasoline Alley.

2

THE INCREDIBLE FLYING MACHINE

M el pulled into the Ormond Garage Parking lot and was
instantly impressed by the number and quality of race
cars. There were racing Corvettes of course, but there were also
Mercedes, Ferrari, Porsch, and Aston Martins, filling the lot.

Lois looked at Mel drooling over the cars and said, "OH, now
Mel." Then, Lois got out of the car and walked towards the garage
office.

Mel knew when he'd been had, so he got out and followed Lois
inside.

Lois and Mel entered the garage, and Mel instantly noticed the
cars inside the garage were even better than the ones outside.
There was a desk just inside the door, and the rest was an open
workspace with at least a dozen exotic race cars scattered around
being worked on.

Lois explained to the person at the desk that they had an
appointment with the owner to discuss changing the garage insurance policy due to the new cars and possible insurance risk from

the fuel they kept on the premises. The lady at the desk called the owner over and introduced Mel and Lois.

After talking with the owner, who was named Doc, for a few minutes and checking out the areas in the shop the insurance company would like to address with changes to the policy, Mel realized there was no flying machine inside, and he had not seen it outside. They needed to see the machine so he and Lois could make their assessment for the FBI, so he took a different approach.

Mel told Doc he was hoping the flying craft was in the garage so he could get a glimpse at it, but he didn't see it and asked if they could see what the big press release was about. Doc got really excited when Mel asked if they could see it, which, of course, was the idea for asking, so he answered yes. The owner told them it was too big for the garage, so they built a large shed out back to keep it out of the weather and prying eyes. The large shed turned out to be a 40-foot by 60-foot steel building. The flying craft they supposedly built was at least 20 feet wide by 40 feet long and looked more like an oblong tube than a flying machine.

The thing in the building in no way resembled a flying machine. If anything, it looked like a flattened submarine without windows, and it was completely smooth. There wasn't any sign of windows, doors, or even a seam in any part of the body. It was as though the thing in front of them was a silver-colored, flattened glass tube with no markings.

Mel was staring at the silver thing, trying to figure out what it really was, when Lois asked, "So where did you find this, and what makes you think this is a flying machine?"

Doc looked at Lois, but before he could say another word, Lois said, "From the looks of this thing, it would have been impossible for you to make it for many reasons, but why do you insist it is a flying machine?"

Doc seemed shocked that Lois would say that so quickly, but after seeing the craft, it was evident the boys at the garage hadn't built it. Mel and Lois then explained to Doc that they were there to check out the flying machine, and they were actually from the FBI.

3

THE APE AND THE FLYING MACHINE

"So, you're from the FBI?" Doc said, "well, I feel better already. We wanted to come clean anyway because this is too much of a secret for us to keep." he added.

Doc said Lois was right; they didn't build the flying machine; they found it. We were test-driving our car down a dirt road just a few miles out in the swamp. The car made no noise, and we didn't want anyone to see our new invention, so we drove out of town to test it. We thought it would make a great city car because it was so quiet, and we wanted to test it in privacy before we announced our plans to make them so no other car maker could steal our ideas.

Everything was going great. The car was faster than anything they had ever built and was completely silent, which is why the trouble started. The car was so silent that within the first few minutes, we almost hit two deer that didn't hear us coming. We slowed it down a bit in the curves to avoid hitting any, and things went perfectly for a few more miles until we came around a corner a bit too fast and hit something.

The driver and I only saw a big furry animal standing on two legs as they came sliding around the corner, and then we hit it. We figured we were doing 60 miles per hour when we hit the animal. It was bigger than any bear we had ever seen, and the collision totaled the race car. Race cars have thin bodies, and they are light, so when we hit the big animal, it destroyed the car. The only reason we were not hurt was that it was a race car. A race car had roll bars, and 5-point harnesses, and we were wearing helmets.

When the car had stopped and the dust settled, both of us men were unhurt. The car was totaled, and we were going to be walking back to the garage. After we got untangled from the wreckage, we looked at the car and couldn't believe one animal could do that much damage to our car. After looking at what was left of the racing car, we started looking for the body of the animal we hit. There was blood on the car and some drips leading away from the wreck, but we could not find a body. That meant there was an injured animal out there, and it was possibly a very big bear from the size of it. Neither of us had a gun; if it was an injured bear, we needed to get out of there quickly. We decided to walk back to the shop get a few guns, and head back out to find the injured animal before it found and injured somebody.

It took two hours to hike back to the garage. After grabbing our best hunting rifles and gathering a few more guys from the shop to help, we drove back to where we hit the animal. The car was still where we left it, and after a quick inspection, we followed the blood trail in hopes of finding the injured animal. Everyone was cautious, fearing it may be an injured bear, so they weren't making a sound as they searched.

Following the blood trail was easy because the wounded animal wasn't losing much blood and most likely wouldn't die from the wound, but it could be dangerous if it were a bear. The men followed the blood for over a mile when they came to a cave. The blood led right into the cave. This was a worst-case scenario if it was a wounded bear, and being that it went into a cave, there was a near 100% chance it was a bear. None of them had a flashlight or lantern, so they had one of the men walk back to the trucks and get lights while the rest of the guys kept guard over the cave's opening.

After the guy returned with lanterns and flashlights, they prepared to enter the cave. The plan was that two guys would hold the lanterns, and their handguns, while the guys with the high-powered rifles would stand next to them in the event it is an injured bear, and it attacked them. Two other guys would enter on the sides with the flashlights taped to their rifles, so they had light to see.

The men entered the cave slowly so their eyes could get accustomed to the low light. As they walked deeper into the cave, they began to notice it was beginning to get lighter. It was almost like there was a light ahead, so they turned their lights off and walked slowly around the corner with all guns ready. The sight that greeted them wasn't a wounded bear but a huge cave that had a glowing light in the ceiling. One of the men suggested it was a glowing moss, but he couldn't be sure. The glowing ceiling wasn't the weirdest thing in the cave they saw. Right in the middle of the cave was a large silver tube. They expected to find a wounded bear and instead found a cave with a glowing ceiling and a large silver tube inside, with no sight of any wounded animal.

While looking at the shiny tube, the men kept vigilant for the wounded animal. They were shining their lanterns and flashlights around the cave when one of the men called out. He had found the animal, but it wasn't a bear, and he wasn't sure what it was. The man who had found the animal kept his light and gun on it until the others were by his side. With the added light from the other lanterns and flashlights they could tell it wasn't a bear, deer, or any other animal they expected. The wounded animal was inside a small nook in the cave, leaning against the wall, holding its hurt and bloody arm. The animal looked like a very tall gorilla.

The ape thing wasn't moving, and one of the men exclaimed it looked friendly just hurt. He was right. The ape had not made a move since they had spotted it. It seemed calm but nervous. One of the men suggested they stop shining all the lights on it and back up to give it space. As soon as they stopped shining the lights on its face, it seemed to relax. As the men backed away, it relaxed even more. As the men backed further away, the ape sat on the floor and cradled its hurt arm.

As the ape sat down, one of the guys called out and asked if Doc was going to fix up the monkey. A couple more guys piped up, teasing their buddy they called Doc about fixing the monkey. It didn't take long before one of the men set his gun on the cave floor and slowly approached the wounded ape thing.

As he walked towards the ape, the man said, "Hi, my name is Doc, and I want to see if I can help you."

"Don't be afraid, I won't hurt you," he added as he got within 5 feet of the ape, then stopped.

The ape looked at him, slowly nodded its head in understanding, then held its injured arm out to Doc. Doc wasn't a Doctor, but he had been fixing his hunting buddies' injuries his whole life, so all his friends called him Doc. Doc looked at the offered arm and could tell it was not broken but had a bad cut. The cut wasn't bleeding too badly, but it needed stitches. Doc looked at the arm and touched it, then touched his hip pack, hoping the ape understood he was trying to help. Later, Doc would say it was the eyes of the ape that made him feel confident he would be okay treating it. The ape watched as Doc removed his first aid gear from his hip pack.

Doc asked one of the guys to bring him a lantern so he could see better. Not one of the tough hunters was brave enough, until the ape pointed at one of the guys, and waved him forward. The whole group of guys gasped in shock. The man with the lantern slowly approached, and the ape slowly lowered its head as if to say thank you. The man held out the lantern and stared at the ape in wonder.

With better light, Doc was able to clean the arm wound and inspect the damage. The whole time, the ape remained calm and never moved, although it watched everything Doc did. Sure enough, the arm wasn't broken, but the cut could really use stitches if the ape would let him. Otherwise, he would try to bandage it. Doc pulled out his suturing kit and showed it to the ape. He showed it the needle with the thread attached, pretended to suture his arm, and then pointed to the ape's arm. To Doc's amazement, the ape closed its eyes, nodded a couple of times, drew a deep breath, and then held out its arm.

The ape never flinched or moved while Doc did the stitching. Doc had stitched quite a few men, and almost everyone flinched or cried out a bit. This ape was not only incredibly calm, but it also never moved until Doc had finished. When Doc finished stitching the arm, he wrapped it with gauze to keep it clean. The ape slowly opened its eyes and touched the bandaged arm. A smile crossed its face, and it gently laid a hand on Doc's shoulder. Then Doc and the ape stood up. Doc was a bit over 6 feet tall, but the ape was at least 2 feet taller. The ape also looked old. It reminded Doc of a silverback gorilla with all the silver hair, but the body hair was longer, and this ape was much taller. In fact, this ape was built more like a human than an ape, he thought. As soon as the ape started walking, Doc realized it even walked like a human, a very tall hairy human, he mused.

Once Doc was done bandaging him, the ape stood up and walked over to the end of the silver tube. Everyone relaxed and watched it walk now that they weren't afraid of it and were curious what it was up to. The ape looked at Doc and then pushed the silver tube. The tube moved as easily as if a child pushed a helium balloon. The ape walked to the other end of the tube, which was still slowly floating, put his hand on it, and it stopped. Then it pushed it back again towards Doc. As the tube reached Doc, he reached out and, with a light touch, stopped the tube. One of the guys had dropped to his knees, shined a flashlight under the tube, saw it was floating, and told Doc.

Doc wasn't a doctor, but he did have years of engineering experience and was one of the best racing mechanics around. Still, he couldn't understand how this tube could be floating unless it was some sort of weather helium balloon this ape found. How it got into this cave is another guess. After closer inspection, Doc realized it wasn't a weather balloon because it was solid like a tube. It also didn't take a genius to see that if the tube was solid, it could not have fit through the cave opening. How it got into the cave was a wonder. How long it had been in the cave was a bigger wonder. What the ape had to do with the tube may be the biggest wonder. It was like the ape felt the tube was his property, and he was showing it off.

Doc knew he needed to take this silver tube back to the garage. Or maybe not until they built a storage building for it because it certainly wouldn't fit into their garage. This thing had to be 20 feet wide, at least 40 feet long, and way over 10 feet tall. There was no doubt in his mind they needed a bigger building. They needed to keep it out of sight until they could figure out what it was and to keep it from blowing away. Doc was still wracking his brain, trying to figure out how this thing could be acting like it had antigravity.

Doc suggested they head back to the garage and build a big shed to house this thing. He was laughing, thinking that all they would need to take it to the garage was a big fishing net and a truck to pull it like a kid pulling a balloon on a string.

Doc looked at the ape thing and asked it to follow him using hand signals. Doc climbed into the back of a pickup and signaled for the ape to join him. Much to Doc's pleasure, the ape climbed in and sat next to him. Doc could tell this wasn't a normal ape, and it seemed smart, so he wanted it back at the garage so he could study it. Once back at the garage, Doc set up a room for the ape in the back storeroom. Doc wasn't married and volunteered to stay in the shop with the ape until they decided what to do while building the new shed.

If they were going to bring in the ape's silver tube, they needed to build a shed as soon as possible. Luckily, they owned the land behind the garage, and they could build it without anyone seeing them. The best part was that the dirt test road they would bring the silver tube in on came through their backfield, which meant if they brought it in at night, no one would know.

It took two weeks to build the shed and another week to prepare to bring the tube back. Doc had them drive a backhoe out to the cave to enlarge the opening and then drape the tube in a strong fishing net. Once everything was ready, they towed the tube one moonless night. The ape always went on trips to the tube and was a great help getting the net over it. Once the tube was safely in the shed, the ape set up his own quarters near it and has never left its side for the last ten years.

"Wait, the ape is here?" asked Lois.

"Why yes, it is, and it has been watching us the whole time from over there." Said Doc.

4

LOIS AND MEL MEET THE APE

Lois and Mel turned to where Doc was pointing, and a very tall hairy ape quietly stood in a doorway. After hearing Doc's story, Mel and Lois weren't sure if he was pulling their legs, and now here was what looked like the tall ape in his story.

Lois looked at the ape thing, knowing possibly one part of the story was real, then said, "I see you have an ape thing, but why do you call this tube a flying machine?"

"But it is a flying machine," said Doc, then he walked over to the silver tube and gave it a little shove.

Much to Mel and Lois's surprise, the large silver tube easily floated across the shed, hit the other side, and gently bounced back towards them. Mel stepped forward and pushed the tube, which easily moved like a balloon. Mel then knelt down and looked under the tube.

"This is unbelievable." Mel stated, then he stood up, shaking his head.

Lois knelt down to have a look for herself, and her reaction was the same as Mel's.

"Mel, I think this is the moment we need the equipment in the car." Lois said, then she began walking around the floating tube.

By this point, Mel and Lois had completely forgotten the tall ape thing, and all they cared about was checking out the fantastic floating tube.

Mel drove the car to the back where the shed was and began unloading the equipment into the shed. Lois continued her inspection of the floating thing, and after she circled the whole thing, she asked for a ladder. The top of the floating craft was 14 feet off the ground, so they brought her a 16-foot-tall folding ladder. Lois climbed the ladder and looked at about 20 feet of the area when she saw an indented handprint. Actually, there were two hand-shaped impressions about 10 feet off the ground, and out of sight, up over the curve of the craft. One was huge, and one was human size. Without thinking, Lois placed her hand into the human-sized indentation, and the reaction was instant.

As soon as Lois placed her hand, a crack appeared on the side of the tube below the impression, and then the side slid down and formed a ramp that went from the side of the tube to the ground. There was one small problem with the ramp sliding down to the ground. Lois's ladder was in the way, and it was pushed out from under her by the ramp opening. It could have been tragic, and Lois could have gotten hurt, but as soon as she started falling toward the tube, her descent slowed and almost stopped. It seemed the closer she approached the craft, the slower she went. It was as if the ship had a force field, so she couldn't hit it very fast.

Mel was coming in the shed doorway as Lois placed her hand into the depression, so he was too far away to help, but he watched with fascination as she slowly descended into the opening and ended up standing upright. From where he was standing, Mel could see inside the tube, and it was a sight to see. The inside was fully lit, and there were blinking lights that looked like gages, but what stood out most was that the doorway into the craft was 10 feet tall. As Mel walked to the tube, he thought it didn't seem to make sense that there would be a door so big in any type of craft unless whoever piloted it was huge.

As Mel and Doc stared with wonder at Lois inside the open tube, the ape, who had been quietly standing aside while Mel and Lois were inspecting, slowly approached. Mel was walking up the ramp to the tube when he noticed the ape standing next to the ramp. Mel stopped in shock, suddenly seeing a huge ape standing 2 feet away.

At that moment, Lois saw the ape standing so close to Mel and let out a little, "Watch out, Mel."

Before Mel or Lois could react, both Doc and the ape began laughing. Lois and Mel stared at Doc and the giant ape laughing, then began shaking their heads.

Doc stopped laughing and said, "I forgot to tell you that the ape here is very friendly. He seems to be smart, and in the ten years he has been here, he has never caused a problem." "He seems to understand a lot, but he doesn't talk," added Doc.

As if on cue, the ape said, "I have stayed here watching over the ship, learning your language, and waiting until one of you could make the ship work like in the past."

Doc stared wide-eyed at the ape that he had lived around for ten years, and said, "well, that was unexpected!" "You are indeed one smart ape," Doc Added.

The ape laughed at Doc's reaction and said, "I have known how to speak your language for a few years, but there was really no reason to talk until today when Lois figured out how to open the ship." "I am charged with protecting the ship until humans return and can run it again." The ape added.

"If I hadn't heard of giant hairy ape-men in my Native American studies, I wouldn't believe this ape was real," said Mel. "The

Native American tribes had many names for them, but the one I remember most is Sasquatch," Mel added.

"I do remember that name in my people's history," said Nani. "There were many names and tribes back then when we were two peoples working and flying together," Nani added.

"You keep calling it a ship," said Mel. "How do you know it is a ship? What kind of ship is it, where did it come from? OH, wait, I am sorry, it is just that this is fantastic," Mel added.

"I am the keeper of my people's knowledge," Nani said. "This ship is part of our history and human history as well," Nani added.

After Nani talked, no one spoke for almost a full minute. Then Lois came to the ship's opening, looked at Nani, and asked what he meant that humans and his people shared history.

Nani sat on the ship's ramp, put his palm to his face, took a deep breath, and said, "I suppose it is time to teach you both of our people's shared history."

Doc, Mel, and Lois listened for the next 2 hours as Nani told of how humans and his people had worked together for thousands of years until a great calamity happened. The humans and we Sasquatch built many fantastic cities and achieved much greater technological levels than humans have today. Luckily, there was sufficient notice about when the disaster from space would happen, so we built many of these ships to help rebuild. We did not fully anticipate how bad the impact from space would be and were caught off guard. Most of our bases and cities were destroyed in the first few hours. Humans and we Sasquatch were plunged into the Stone Age, many thousands of years. It is only these last few decades that humans have advanced enough that you will be able to fly the ship.

A few bases survived the impact and decided to send these ships to all corners of the earth to await when we could pick ourselves back up. When Doc accidentally hit me 10 years ago, I realized we were getting close to the point where a human could run the ship again, so I came along and kept silent until today.

Before the great flood, the Sasquatch and humans worked and traveled in these ships as teams. Nani explained he only knew the history of their two peoples and how they worked together, but all the knowledge of both their peoples before the great flood was stored in this ship. This ship is a library of our complete knowledge to be shared when my people and humans reunite. Nani explained that there were more of these ships in caves around the world, all waiting for humans to advance enough to make them work again.

Nani explained that humans were the ships' pilots, and his people were the helpers and mechanics. He joked that only humans could fly ships because the controls were too small for his people to use. Then Nani said seriously that only humans had the mental ability to bond or join with the navigational system of the ships. Nani then laughed again and said his people were always too lazy to learn to pilot and thought it was easier to have humans fly them around and fix what they broke.

Lois looked at Nani and asked him if this ship could still fly. Nani told her indeed it could, but he felt its best use was as a learning center because it contained all the knowledge needed to free his people and help humans advance to where they were thousands of years ago. He added that this ship and the others like it can also fly in space.

Lois looked at Mel and said, we need to test the flying machine to see if it is the real thing." "I'm not saying the talking ape is lying, but we need to try this ship, and if it is the real deal, then we need to get it to the FBI as soon as possible." Lois added.

Nani smiled at Lois, thinking how funny her hard-hitting humor was. Then, they agreed that they should see if they could figure out how to run the ship again. Mel nodded in agreement as well, walked up the ramp onto the ship, and stood by Lois, looking around the inside of the ship. Nani walked up the ramp behind Mel, and as soon as the Sasquatch stepped inside the ship, the ship's systems came to life. The cabin lights came on, and various panels opened to reveal electric equipment like Lois and Mel had never seen before. Doc came in last, shaking his head at what he was seeing.

Nani explained he did not have any idea how the ship worked. He was one of many Knowledge Keepers waiting for thousands of years until a human could open it. Nani remembered that there was something in the stories about waiting for a human that was advanced enough and had the special ability to pilot the ship. It was obvious Lois had a special ability since she was able to open the ship. Nani went on to explain that the ship also needs a Sasquatch to fully operate. A human or a Sasquatch could access the library at any time alone, but to fly the ship requires a human pilot and a Sasquatch to complete the biological circuit necessary to operate it.

"I knew you were wired differently, Lois, but I didn't know it meant you could fly a spaceship with a giant monkey as your co-pilot." Mel said, then jumped away from Lois's swinging tool bag.

"I must remind you that, although I have spent 50 years guarding this ship, I have never been in it until now, so I am as lost as the rest of you as to how things work," Nani said. "I only know my presence inside the ship is required for you to fully understand all the systems," Nani added, then he walked around the ship looking.

"I think we need to do a full survey of the outside and inside of the ship, plus we should determine the full extent of the ship's capabilities before we report back to the FBI," Mel stated, then he too began walking around the ship checking things out with the Sasquatch.

Lois watched Mel and the Sasquatch walk around like they were best friends. She still doubted that an ape could talk, let alone be trusted not to get mad and hurt her. Nani was an 8-foot-tall fur-covered ape, or Sasquatch as he is called, and Mel walked around with it like he had been doing it for years. She was never going to figure out men. She thought that she better find out what Nani eats just to be sure, then she too began searching inside the ship.

5

DISCOVERING THE SHIPS ABILITIES

U nder the circumstances, Doc canceled all the press announcements and showing for the flying machine. He told the newspaper the flying machine had been damaged beyond repair in a fire, and they were not sure if they would rebuild it again. That would allow them the time and privacy to inspect the ship and determine if it could actually fly. Since it was already floating, the possibility that it could fly was rather high, thought Mel. However, the fact that the Sasquatch said Lois was the only one who was biologically able to fly the ship made him nervous. She couldn't parallel park their car, and the Sasquatch expected her to fly the ship. Now, he wished they really sold insurance.

Over the next three days, they checked every button, panel, and screen around the ship. They used masking tape and a pen to label the things they figured out. They found the library, but the language was not in English, so figuring out the systems was of no help. Lois and Mel have been around TV's, but the TV screens on the ship were very different and almost clear until the message or picture was on them.

There was one scary moment when Lois placed her hand into a hand-shaped impression on one end of the ship. Once she placed her palm flat, the area around her opened up and turned into a pilot's station. Even a pilot's chair came out of the floor so she could sit. The whole end of the ship became as clear as a window, and she could see through and see the inside of the shed the ship was in. After the pilot's station was locked into place, the sides of the ship began turning into windows that you could see the shed through as well.

Mel walked outside the ship and began walking completely around it. When he came back to the ship, he let everyone know he could not see windows from the outside. In fact, it was very hard to see the ship at all. It was as though the ship turned almost invisible, and what you could make out still looked like a flattened silver tube without windows. That meant whoever was flying this ship could fly around, and no one would know who was flying it, that is if they could see it at all. Mel thought if this thing were flying fast, it would be invisible.

Lois and Mel were wondering how to fly it and how fast it was. If it was fast and invisible, the FBI would go crazy when they heard about it. If the ship was a big enough deal for the FBI, it might even get them a cushy assignment in Mexico or somewhere other than wet Washington State. There was no other option than to test it before they told their FBI bosses so they couldn't steal their thunder.

On the fourth day, Lois said she was ready to try flying the ship. Over the last 2 days they were able to hover the ship higher, lower, forward, back, left and right, and they found the throttle increasing speed. Lois said she knew what every flight control button, leaver and screen did, except the group of 7 blinking-colored switches on a separate panel next to the steering lever. Nothing happened when she pressed them in the shed, so she assumed they had something to do with in-flight controls. They would have to be flying the ship to test them.

Mel told Lois he wasn't in so much of a hurry that they couldn't check those switches a bit closer, so they didn't have to take a chance on the fly. "I mean, what if those buttons shoot guns or mistles?" said Mel.

"OH, come on, Mel, where's your spirit of adventure?" said Lois.

"I lost it when I said, 'I Do,' to a redhead," Mel said, then ducked knowing something would come flying.

Nani smiled at the banter between Mel and Lois, then said he agreed with Lois that it was time to test fly the ship.

Doc told them, "There was no time like the present to test it," and opened the shed doors.

"Looks like I am outvoted in this democracy," said Mel as he smiled at Lois and gave her a thumbs up.

Lois sat in the pilot's seat and ran the systems up-to-full flight prep. Nani closed the ship's ramp while Mel sat in the co-pilot's seat. Once Doc had the shed doors fully opened, Lois eased the ship through the shed doors and into the open air. Lois wanted to run through a few tests outside the shed before she tried flying. She was worried what the wind would do to the lighter-than-air ship. After a few minutes in the wind, it was determined the craft held its position regardless of the wind speed. Lois tried maneuvering the craft to get used to the controls. She had the ship rise, move to the left, move to the right, then return to its original position.

Lois knew that flying the ship was going to take practice. The things that will be especially important to practice will be steering, adjusting the speed, and changing altitude. The controls seem to be done by electric current because they could find no cables or other things required for normal airplanes to fly. Nani suggested that the ship would mostly fly itself if their folklore could be believed. Most of the controls seemed to be controlled by some sort of very advanced computer. The information screens were like thin, transparent plastic that lit up like a TV screen when turned on, but the language, as expected, wasn't in English.

With luck, due to his education, to be the Knowledge Keeper, Nani, learned to read his people's forgotten language, so he could read most of the language that was written on the ship and on the screens, and he taught Lois what the numbers meant on the instruments she needed to fly the ship. Lois said she really only needed the altitude and speed indicators deciphered in order for her to fly. Mel wasn't too happy that the pilot of the ship he was flying on couldn't read the instruments and tried insisting they wait until Lois could read all the gauges and instruments. Mel didn't get any mileage out of his complaining, so he clammed up and prepared for their first flight.

Once Lois was sure the controls were operating properly, she had Nani make one of the ships' windows normally hidden from the outside transparent, and he signaled Doc to let him know they were taking off. Doc waved goodbye, and Lois flew the craft to an altitude of 500 feet to make sure she would clear any trees in the area, then began flying towards the beach. Lois thought that nothing in the whole state of Florida was taller than a couple hundred feet, so they would be safe flying anywhere at that height, no matter what speed.

6

FLYING THE SILVER SHIP

L ois slowly inched the ship speed faster so she could become accustomed to the controls in flight. Nani let Lois know he could feel no sensation of moving as she increased the ship's speed. Once Lois had the ship moving at a few hundred miles an hour out over the ocean, she ran a few tests. The ship was almost invisible, but they didn't want to take a chance they would be seen while they were testing the ship, so they were doing their testing over the Atlantic Ocean. After doing a few fast vertical and horizontal maneuvers, Nani announced that there was no feeling of movement or any inertia of any kind inside the ship while it was moving. Mel couldn't explain how it was possible that they couldn't feel any movement unless the ship somehow controlled gravity. After satisfying herself that they weren't going to feel motion, Lois decided to run the ship through a few extreme maneuvers to see what would happen. At one point, Lois told Nani and Mel to take a glance out of the front of the ship.

Without saying a word to her passengers, Lois had dropped the altitude of the ship to 10 feet off the water and was flying upside down when Mel and Nani glanced out the front window. To make things worse, they were still flying about 200-MPH and on a collision course with a large cargo ship. Lois wanted to scare Mel and Nani by doing a close flyby of the cargo ship. Suddenly, while they were flying directly at the cargo ship, their ship made an evasive maneuver and flew vertically for about 1000 feet, leveled off, flew over the ship, then flew back down to flying 10 feet of the water.

Mel and Nani actually screamed when they saw the cargo ship approaching them while they were upside down. Lois even let out a bit of a scream when the ship surprised her and reacted on its own to avoid hitting the cargo ship. After the ship returned to its original flying position, everyone let out a big sigh, then Lois took over the controls again and flew the ship back to 500 feet off the ocean again and right side up as well.

"Well, now we know the ship can fly itself," said Lois. "I was going to give you two a bit of a scare, but the ship had a mind of its own." She added.

Lois explained to Mel and Nani how she was testing the artificial gravity and inertial control by flying upside down, and they hadn't felt it when she saw the cargo ship. She decided to show them how quickly the ship moved and to show they wouldn't feel it inside the ship. She was about to fly their ship over the cargo ship when their ship took over the controls and avoided the cargo ship on its own.

"I, for one, am amazed," said Nani, "But next time, please warn us if you are going to test the ship's systems with such vigor because I almost lost my lunch," Nani said, then chuckled.

"Really Lois!" Mel said, glaring at Lois. "That stunt took 20 years off my life, and my heart will take a week to slow down," added Mel while he made a slightly annoyed face.

After things calmed down on the ship, Nani said he had been

watching one of the screens that had 7 blinking lights and one of the blinking lights had been moving since we took off. He read the screen and decided the light moving was them in their ship, and the other lights were ships like the one they were on. Lois suggested Nani try adjusting the screen to see if they could get more detail and information.

While Nani checked the screen, Lois and Mel discussed the ship. Mel was certain the FBI was going to be impressed beyond belief at this ship, and if there were six more just like it, he and Lois would have written their future with the FBI in gold. If there were seven ships like this, and Nani is correct that his people, the Sasquatch, and humans worked together, then there would be a massive amount of political maneuvering before things iron out, especially for the Sasquatch. Lois told Mel she was worried that humans would hurt the Sasquatch. Mel told her that they had to trust their bosses at the FBI, which didn't make her feel any better.

Nani announced he had finished studying the screen, and indeed, it was a map, or more precisely, a model of the earth, and it looked like it was real. Lois and Mel walked to where Nani was standing, and sure enough, the screen was now showing a three-dimensional view of the earth, with seven blinking lights spread around the globe. One blinking light was moving; on closer inspection, it was off the coast of Florida, according to the map.

Nani pointed at the moving light and said it was them, and the other six were spread around the earth. Lois looked at the map and saw a blinking light in Washington state and suggested they head that way and test this ship's speed. If it could fly into space, it should be able to fly to Washington state quickly. Nani also noticed the seven blinking lights were each a different color, and that color matched the seven blinking switches on the panel. Lois couldn't figure out what they did. Nani suggested that the switch had small lettering that he thought said the blinking switch might be a go-to shortcut button.

Lois looked at Nani after he said the blinking switch on her panel was a go-to button and wondered what that meant. Before Mel or Nani could speak or react, Lois touched the blinking button corresponding to the Washington state map location. Mel and Nani had a split second before Lois touched the switch to think about the implications, and all their thoughts ended badly.

It wasn't so much a feeling of movement or the passing of time, but it seemed for a split second, it got pitch black, then suddenly they were not flying over the open ocean off the Florida coast, but over a green forest.

Nani looked at the map with the seven blinking lights and said, "Looks like we are now across the country from Florida and are flying over Washington state." "I can see our light has moved, and if the other blinking light on the map next to ours is another ship, then it is inside that mountain we just stopped in front of." Nani stated, then resumed looking at his map.

"Alright, Lois, I know we are not hurt, and everything is going fine, but can you please let us know before you do stuff like that," said Mel.

"You can't blame me, guys," said Lois. "There is no way anyone could have known what would happen if the switch was pushed because there has never been anything like this before," Lois added.

"And if you impulsively keep doing things, no one may ever learn about this ship because we will be lost somewhere in space," said Mel, a bit annoyed.

"It is interesting you should mention space," said Nani. "I was adjusting the map size and noticed two ships were not on land. One is in the middle of the ocean, and the other is in space."

"Lois, don't get any funny ideas about trying to find the one in space until we determine if this old bucket is still airtight," said Mel.

"I won't push anymore blinking lights if someone can tell me how we traveled over 3000 miles, in a second," Lois said. "I just double-checked the instruments, and we traveled over 3400 miles in less than a second, without the feeling of movement."

"It appears this ship can either travel at the speed of light or bend time and space," announced Mel. "In all my years working in the field of physics, it never dawned on me that humans would ever travel at the speed of light, and I just did," added Mel.

"The best translation I can get from reading the flight manual is that it is called 'the long-distance instant travel setting,' and they say it steps through time and distance to reach its destination," Nani stated. "I do not believe any time passes no matter how far you travel, but it only works when traveling from one of the blinking locations on the map, accessed by pressing the blinking switch as Lois did," Nani added.

"I have 3 Ph.D.s in math, physics, and engineering, and the science behind this is so far above my understanding. I feel like a child watching a magic show," Mel said with a deep sigh.

"Well, with the current limited level of computer science I have been trained on, compared to the computers on this ship that seem to think like humans, I also feel over my head," said Lois. "If it weren't for Nani being able to translate, I wouldn't have been able to turn a light on in this ship, so my stress level is at the top too," Lois said and smiled at Nani.

"OK, we all agree that this is a great ship and might be of great value to Sasquatch, humans, and the FBI, but where is the ship we came to see?" asked Mel.

Nani nodded, turned to the map that showed the blinking

lights, and began adjusting the map. Once they reached their destination, the ship stopped and was hovering in place approximately 500 feet from the face of a tall mountain. Since the ship was not moving, Lois had nothing to do, so she and Mel watched Nani work. After about 5 minutes, Nani made a frustrated sound and stood up.

Once Nani calmed down a bit, he told them he could tell the ship was about 100 feet inside the mountain. He said it appears the ship is in a clear opening, but time has caused a landslide to cover the cave's opening. They would need to come back here with the proper equipment to dig out the opening to reach the ship inside. He added that the ship was in perfect working order, just buried. While he was trying to locate the ship, he was able to link the ship's communication systems so he could check out the other ships' systems. From the readings he received, the ship was fully operational, but there was no sign of a Knowledge Keeper.

Mel laughed and said, "The FBI and the American government would be more than eager to rescue the ship inside the mountain," even if that was not the best move, he was thinking to himself.

Lois agreed with Mel and said she "expected the FBI and the government to be all over these ships as soon as they could get their hands on them."

All the while Lois was talking, Mel was wondering if the kind of power and knowledge these ships had was safe in any government's hands. The hairs on the back of Mel's neck rose every time he thought of someone using these ships for destructive purposes. He wished he had a few of his scientist friends along so they could help determine the best course of action. As much as he loved working for the FBI, he believed that the kind of scientific and historical knowledge to be gained from the ships and Nani would be best addressed by scientists and professionals rather than the government. Mel believed that this was human history being unraveled after meeting Nani and finding the ship, and it should be shared with all humanity, not grabbed and buried by a government, buried, and used for power. All he could do was continue searching for the ships and see how it all came out in the wash.

7

LOOKING TOR THE LAST 5 SHIPS

After looking at the mountain face for a while and thinking in silence, Lois suggested they check out the other ship locations on the map. Nani loved the idea, but Mel quickly suggested they could go home and come back tomorrow.

"Why put off for tomorrow what you could do today?" said Lois. "I think we should check out every ship's location today since travel time is instantaneous, and will not take too long," she added.

"All is fun and games until you push the blinking switch for the ship in outer space," Mel said, then pretended to shake like he was scared.

"I must agree with Lois and believe we should continue looking for the other five ships today," Nani said. "It might not be a bad idea to wait until the very end to look at the two ships that are not on land, so we can verify that our ship is performing well enough to go underwater and into outer space," he added and smiled at Mel.

"I am also fine with waiting until the end for those two ships, not on land, so maybe we should try for the next closest ship," Lois said.

"There is a blinking light out in the ocean on what looks like an island about 2400 miles west of here," said Nani.

"That sounds like the Hawaiian islands," said Mel. "That's 2400 miles across open ocean, which is a bit disconcerting," he added.

"Well, we just traveled a thousand miles further with no problems," said Lois.

"That's right. Three thousand four hundred miles over land, so if there was a problem, we could land on ground, not ocean." Mel stated.

"I think if something goes wrong, it will not matter where we are traveling," said Nani. "Because I believe if something goes wrong during one of the instant travels, there will not be anything left of us to find," Nani said, knowing it was dangerous no matter what they did.

"I agree with Nani," said Lois. "If anything goes wrong, we're goners anyway, so let's give it a try, so we can give a full report to our bosses at the FBI," she added, hovering her hand over the blinking switch for Hawaii.

"OK, you two win, but if we die, I am not talking to either of you ever again," Mel declared, then gave Lois a thumbs up.

Lois's finger touched the blinking switch Nani said was for Hawaii, and again, everything went slightly weird. It wasn't the feeling of a complete blackout, but they felt a bit strange. Then they were suddenly not facing a tree-covered mountain, but an old black lava field, surrounded by palm trees. Upon closer inspection, they were nowhere near any city or town. All they could see were palm trees and the old lava field. Nani was the first to see the cave and pointed it out to Lois so she could fly closer to it.

The cave was about 200 feet up a steep cliff face and would

have been impossible to see if they hadn't been hovering directly in front of the cave opening. You would have missed it even if you were flying by the cave. Lois flew the ship to the cave opening, hovered while she picked the best spot to get out, then opened the ship's door so they could explore.

Nani suggested he lead the party out of the ship. He said since he was very big and strong, if there was any danger, he could protect them. Plus, if there were a Knowledge Keeper in the cave, Nani would need to talk to them before Mel or Lois. Mel thanked him and let him know that there weren't any dangerous animals on the Hawaiian islands, but being there to talk to the other Knowledge Keeper was needed. Nani looked at Mel and said, "Better safe than sorry because I have seen alligators swim quite a long distance, so It might still be a good idea to keep a lookout for them."

Both Lois and Mel held back their laughter at Nani's last comment and allowed him to be their protector. Seriously, who wouldn't want an 8-foot-tall 600-pound Sasquatch as your personal guard as you walk into a cave? Nani didn't take notice or care that he had given Lois and Mel a little humorous delight. Instead, he stood up straight, walked down the ship's ramp onto the black lava, and walked towards the cave. Lois covered her mouth to stifle her giggling and followed Nani down the ramp to the cave. Mel grabbed a couple of flashlights and followed Lois out of the ship. As he walked down the ramp, he thought he would never be able to wipe the silly grin off his face after Nani demanded to protect them from alligators on a mountain in Hawaii.

Mel handed a flashlight to Lois as they entered the cave. Nani let them know his low-light vision was much better than humans, so he didn't need a flashlight unless it was completely dark.

The cave entrance was mostly clear of plant growth, so they

were able to enter easily. Nani immediately noticed that there had not been a Knowledge Keeper in the cave for hundreds of years. As they walked into the cave, Nani told them that the cave was so dirty that it was obvious no one had been in the cave for centuries, not even humans. As they approached the ship, Nani walked to the side of the cave and into a small room. Lois and Mel were inspecting the ship when Nani left the little room and came over to them.

Nani announced that there was no Knowledge Keeper in the cave and had not been for 5 or 6 thousand years. Mel and Lois turned to him and noticed that Nani looked sad or upset. Before either Lois or Mel could ask Nani what was wrong, he told them what he found.

Nani told them he read the diary of the last Knowledge Keeper. The diary discussed a time when the humans and Sasquatch lived here and had many small communities on the islands. One day the diary states, a group of humans arrived by boat, of a different type than the ones on the islands with the Sasquatch. They were not as advanced as the Sasquatch and humans already on the islands. The Knowledge Keeper wrote that the new humans were from a civilization their peoples had not contacted yet, so they were not technologically advanced.

Nani said the diary went to say that the Sasquatch and humans on the island allowed these new people onto the islands and accepted them as friends. Unknown to the Sasquatch and humans already on the island, the new visitors carried diseases to which they had no immunity for. It surprised everyone when the first person got sick six weeks later. Within a week after the first person got sick, 90% of the original humans and Sasquatch on the island were sick. Within a month only a couple dozen of the original Sasquatch and humans had survived. The Knowledge Keeper was one of the originals that didn't get sick because he was here in the cave and wasn't affected by the disease. The Knowledge Keeper wasn't aware of the arrival of the new human visitors because he was on a two-week teaching expedition with the rest of the crew.

The humans and Sasquatch together had defeated diseases centuries earlier, so they had no medical science to combat the new ones these humans brought with them. The Knowledge Keeper learned of the crisis unfolding down the mountain, but also knew there was nothing he could do about it, so he stayed in the cave, away from the humans carrying the diseases. The Knowledge Keeper began to worry after a few months without seeing or hearing from another person. No one had come to visit him or bring him the supplies he needed, and not one visitor had come to his cave for teaching or guidance. He knew it was time he left his cave and did a little bit of exploring. He needed to know what was happening and determine if anyone he knew was still alive.

The Knowledge Keeper told of how, after walking for an hour, he stood on the cliff, looking down at the community below him, and was brought to tears immediately. The scene below was heart-wrenching. Most of the buildings had been burned to the ground, and the Knowledge Keeper knew they were trying to burn the disease in whatever building or home it struck. He looked around the streets below, and the Knowledge Keeper saw the occasional body of one of the last survivors of the horrible disease. When the last few survivors died, there was no one to bury them, so they still lay where they passed after months. According to the medical library on the ship, it would be unsafe for the Knowledge Keeper to venture into the community for months, so he would return to his cave to wait alone.

Before he left for the cave, the Knowledge Keeper looked for signs of the visitors that brought the disease. From his vantage point, he ascertained that the visitors left when his people began getting sick. He believed that the visitors may have left completely because they were afraid of getting sick as well, not knowing they were the ones who brought it in the first place. After scanning the area further, it became apparent the visitors stole everything they could as they left. The Knowledge Keeper could see personal items strewn all over the streets as if someone had emptied the contents of the houses and buildings, looking for precious items. Indeed, the visitors brought the disease, stole their lives, and then stole their things.

The Knowledge Keeper wrote that he lived off the land around the cave, since no more supply runs were coming his way. He lost weight, but it was needed and unavoidable since he spent 4 hours a day browsing for food like a deer. Sasquatch mostly ate plants, and these islands were a tropical greenhouse for plants, so there was no shortage of food. If he wanted a variety of foods to eat, he needed to do a bit of hiking, which kept him in good shape.

After six months, he ventured back to the community to explore. He knew that the disease was gone, so it was safe to see if there was anything he could gather to make his life easier until help arrived. It reminded him that it was taking too long for help to arrive from one of the other six communities. He didn't know what, but he knew something bad would have happened if they hadn't received any outside help in ten months. As he walked, the Knowledge Keeper was still lost in his thoughts, so he didn't see the other Sasquatch until he almost ran into them.

The other Sasquatch looked like it had seen a ghost and was standing staring at the Knowledge Keeper like he was a ghost. It took a few long seconds before either Sasquatch could speak, and it was the Sasquatch that the Knowledge Keeper almost stepped on that broke the silence by asking if he was real. The Knowledge Keeper assured his fellow Sasquatch he was real, then asked what had happened and if there were any more survivors.

The new Sasquatch was one of the older ladies from near

the edge of the community that grew the flowers for the community. She explained that she and two other female Sasquatch who live in the forest had been working on plants deep in the jungle when the visitors arrived. During the fourth week of their work, the supplies stopped being delivered. By the 5th week, one of the other ladies working with us walked back to the community to see the problem. When she came back, she told of all the deaths in the community and that she knew she was sick and remained a safe distance from the three ladies while she talked. After she talked to us, she left, knowing we would never see one another. We waited a few more months until we thought the disease was gone and returned to the community and have been here since.

The Knowledge Keeper and the ladies talked from a distance to ensure they didn't get one another sick. The Knowledge Keeper finished by saying that over the years, the ladies passed, and when it was his time, he prepared the ship for a long wait. Since the Knowledge Keeper assumed the disease traveled around the world and took out most of his civilization, it might be hundreds and maybe thousands of years for someone to find the ship. That means the ship is in perfect working order but will need to be restarted, which can take a week or two to be ready for flight. When Nani told the Knowledge Keepers story, everyone bowed their heads for a prayer.

Lois was the first to speak, saying, "if we can't fly this one, let's move to the next ship's location before the FBI thinks we got lost."

"Look, I fully agree with Lois about going and checking the next location as soon as possible, now that we know this ship is grounded." "I just don't want to go underwater or into space thank you very much," Mel added, putting his hands on his hips and staring at Lois.

"I also must concur that moving on is the best course of

action," said Nani. "Although a bit of weightlessness would be fun," Nani added, and then he poked Mel in the ribs and laughed.

"If not the ocean or outer space, what is our next best target ship?" asked Lois. "And if you want to tease Mel, we can sneak in the outer space one," Lois said to Nani.

"Lois, you know I want to tease Mel, but if we did that, I am sure he would pout, and then we wouldn't get anything done again." Nani said, then he picked Mel up like a feather and said, "Don't worry, Mel, I won't let mean old Lois hurt you."

By the time Nani put Mel down, Lois laughed so hard she was doubled over wheezing. Nani looked at Lois laughing and began laughing, too. Pretty soon, Mel was staring at his two flight companions, who were in no condition to fly, wishing for a new crew.

Once the fun and games ended, Nani suggested the blinking dot in an area Lois said was Italy. She recognized the famous boot shape as he was pointing out the two alternatives other than the ocean or outer space. Mel said he liked spaghetti, so that would be a nice place to try. Lois looked at Mel after he said that and punched the button without warning, hoping it would get Mel back for being silly. They arrived instantly, and where they stopped caused Lois and Mel to pause. Mel was the first to speak, and he mostly said they needed to leave as quickly as possible.

Lois saw what Mel was talking about and suggested Nani give them a different ship's location now! Nani had no idea why Lois and Mel wanted to leave so quickly, but he understood the tone of their voices and the urgency it was presenting.

Nani looked at Lois and said, "Push the silver blinking switch."

Lois pushed the switch, and it felt like they blinked out, then back into existence. Mel was the first to make a noise of total surprise and grunting, followed by Nani, who started laughing almost immediately. Lois was the last one to notice because she was in a chair. Once she started floating, Lois realized they were in outer space.

"Nani, I thought we weren't going into outer space, so why did you have me push that button?" asked Lois.

"To be honest, Lois, I said push the silver blinking switch, and you pushed the white blinking switch, which, as you can tell, is in outer space," said Nani, with a definite big smile, as he started doing somersaults in the new weightlessness.

Lois, Nani, and even Mel, stopped being an adult and played for a bit until Nani suggested they turn on the artificial gravity switch he just saw. Mel fully agreed with having gravity and his feet on the floor, not floating above his head. While they were floating weightlessly, Nani asked Lois and Mel why they had to leave so quickly last time in Europe, Italy.

Mel looked at Nani and explained that there are governments and religions that we shouldn't mess with, and we appeared in front of the Vatican, which is the headquarters of the Catholic church. He told of how big and powerful the church is and that it has been reported that they have traveled the world collecting things from various people. If their ship stopped in front of the Vatican, then it must mean the ship is being held in storage below the Vatican, which means it is unreachable.

Nani thought about what Mel had said for a moment, then said, "I do not understand why anyone would want to hold onto the knowledge on the ship and not share it."

"You know, Nani, if they don't have someone like me who has the advanced biological ability to open the ship, then they may not have ever opened it, so they do not know of its true value," said Lois.

"I hope that is the reason, Lois, because I would hate to think someone would want to hide our history and knowledge," Nani said, then he floated to a panel and began pushing buttons.

Once gravity was restored, Nani found the ship in space. He checked the systems, and as expected, the ship was empty. The log states they took a lifeboat to the surface so the ship could be safely orbiting Earth in space. The problem was that without spacesuits, they couldn't check out the ship. Nani completed a systems check and found it would be fine in its current orbit for thousands more years, which would give Mel and Lois's FBI plenty of time to come back and get the ship.

"That means four ships down, counting the one we are in, with 2 to go, so it was time to move on to the next ship." Suggested Nani.

"Again, I am all for checking out the next ship, but can we all please be sure what color-blinking switch we suggest and push this time," said Mel. "If I look out the window and see a shark, I promise I will scream, loud and long," Mel added, then held on for the next shift.

Lois and Nani were careful and made sure Lois pushed the correct button. They came out above dry land and not under the sea, so Mel was relieved, but their location was strange. The map showed that they were in the middle of the Nevada desert. The strange part was the blinking switch Lois pushed was supposed to be in South America. And to complicate things even more, it appeared they were above some sort of military base.

Lois and Nani each reviewed their maps and screens multiple times and found that they were above a Nevada desert. Nani suggested that the blinking lights had shown the original location, and when Lois pushed the switch, they were transported to the ship's current location. Once he finished telling Mel and Lois what he thought, Nani turned and began scanning a screen while Mel and Lois stared at the base below.

They had been floating above the Nevada desert military base for approximately five minutes when Lois noticed four blinking lights moving fast across one of her screens. She showed them to Mel, who after a few seconds, suddenly swore out loud.

"OH, my dear, I think those lights are incoming military intercepting jets," said Mel in an urgent voice. "And, if I'm correct, they are coming to intercept us," he added.

Nani looked at Lois's screen, then adjusted the one he was standing at before explaining what he found. Nani told them that he had learned someone must have moved the ship from its original position, as shown by the blinking lights. Once they tried moving the ship without Lois's ability to connect with the ships, the ship would shut down and secure itself from entry. Simply put, until someone like Lois places their hand on the ship, it will remain locked, and there isn't anything humans possess that can open it, let alone scratch the surface. Nani told them he wished he had a way to watch the frustration the humans were having trying to open it. Nani had barely finished his sentence when the four jets reached their location, then flew past at full speed like they hadn't seen them.

"Well, that was unexpected," said Mel. "I assumed they would radio us, then warn us or tell us to land, but they flew by like we didn't exist," Mel added with a confused look.

"I'm not a pilot, but I don't think the jets were flying so fast they couldn't have seen us," said Lois.

"I might be responsible for that," chimed in Nani. I took the liberty of completely cloaking us from their instruments, and at their speed, they wouldn't have seen us as near transparent as our ship is." Nani added with a big grin.

The jets came back three times, looking for any trace of them, before Mel suggested they get out of there. After discussing the dangers, even Mel agreed that trying the underwater ship's location was safe now that they had tested the ship in outer space, so Lois pushed its blinking switch. In an instant, the ship was underwater, or at least Mel hoped they were, because it was totally dark, and there was no way to tell where they were.

Nani made a few adjustments to his screen, and the area in front of the ship lit up like a football field in a night game. Once the ships' lights came on, they could see they were directly in front of a cave. Nani told Lois to slowly enter the cave while he linked with the ship inside. Lois piloted the ship into the cave opening, which was more than four times bigger than theirs. After 200 feet, the cave opened into a huge cavern. Nani told Lois the cavern had a base with breathable air just 100 feet above them and to surface.

Nani wasn't lying about a cavern or a base. The cavern was the size of a small city, and Lois could see why the cave entrance was so large. Scattered around the cavern were dozens of ships similar to theirs. Some were smaller, some were huge, and must have barely fit through the cave entrance. Lois and Mel looked around the cavern while Nani was busily working his screen.

After 10 minutes, Nani sat back, let out a big sigh, then told them that all the ships logs indicate that the disease that took out the base in Hawaii reached here as well and finally killed the last humans and Sasquatch based here. Before the last few survivors passed away, they secured the base and ships for an extended period, knowing that it could take quite some time before anyone was able to come back.

After Nani finished speaking, he leaned back in his chair for a few moments, then said, "There is nothing here for us, so we might as well go back home and let the FBI experts sort all these ships out."

Lois and Mel could hear the pain and disappointment Nani was feeling. His life had been spent waiting for a human to help him with his ship and to find the other ships and their Knowledge Keepers, but it turns out he is the last Knowledge Keeper. Lois was all for heading back home and giving this ship and the others to the FBI, hoping for a great bonus and maybe a perfect new job. Mel didn't say so, but he was having his doubts that these ships and the technology that comes with them is something he would trust the FBI with or even any government.

After Nani downloaded all the information from the ships in the cavern, he let Lois know he was ready to head back. Lois looked at Mel, who reluctantly gave a thumbs up, and Lois began piloting their ship back out of the cavern where it would be safe. As Lois was piloting the ship back out into the open water, Nani informed her that she would have to manually pilot the ship back home until he figured out how to return home with instant travel when not going to another ship.

A few minutes later, Lois had them back outside the cavern and ready to return, so Nani suggested she pilot the ship to the surface and begin heading home in manual flight mode. Once Lois reached the surface, Nani suggested she fly the ship 50 feet above the ocean and head towards North Florida. The map showed they were in the Atlantic Ocean, South of Florida, 100 miles East of the Falkland Islands. All Lois needed to do was fly north around South America to reach Florida, and she would never fly over any land, so an altitude of 50 feet would mean there wasn't anything they could hit.

The trip was going well, and Lois decided to increase the ship's speed so they could get home and eat dinner. They all had missed lunch, and she was about to faint from hunger, so she increased the speed even more. Neither Mel nor Nani was paying attention to Lois's flying because the ship's gravitational controls made it smooth in the ship no matter how she flew. Lois now had the ship's speed almost maxed out, and the ocean was flying by when a buzzer started sounding.

Nani immediately called out to Lois when he saw what was happening. The buzzer indicated they were approaching Florida, but they were going too fast to stop at their destination. Nani was trying to tell Lois what she needed to do when she accidentally pushed a switch with her elbow while she was reaching across the panel to the screen. The ship's change of direction was instantaneous, and they dove down and slammed into the ground, then cartwheeled a few dozen times before coming to rest.

When the ship came to rest, all systems were down, and Nani, Mel, and Lois were in a heap at one end of the ship. When the ship hit the ground, the inertial gravitational systems failed, but luckily, they failed slowly, or everyone in the ship would have been crushed against the ship when it hit. Nani had held Lois and Mel as they tumbled, protecting them with his body. Nani slowly pushed the loose items that had landed on them during the ship's somersaulting, off their bodies and helped Mel up. Lois was unconscious, and Nani carried her over to a clear area where he could lay her down.

Lois was out cold but not bleeding. Mel and Nani made sure each other was unhurt. The ship's systems held just long enough to save their lives, but now all systems on the ship were dead. Nani went over to the ship's exit ramp and manually opened the ship, so they could go outside. Once outside, Nani Informed Mel that before they crashed, they had gotten within 5 miles of the Ormond garage where they started, so Lois wasn't too far off the mark.

After double checking Lois wasn't in danger of dying, Nani picked her up, cradled her like a baby, and told Mel they were walking to the Garage as quickly as possible so Lois could go to the hospital.

After Nani carried Lois back to the Ormond Garage, Doc and Mel took her to the hospital; Nani disappeared and was never seen again. Nani knew humans weren't ready for the ships and the knowledge they contained, so he and his Sasquatch troupe moved the ship from where it crashed and into a new cave far from humans, at least until they were ready for such knowledge and power.

When Lois regained consciousness, it was found that she had lost her memory for the last week. She remembered leaving for Ormond Garage but not arriving, and she absolutely had no memory of the ship of Nani the Sasquatch. Mel thought it was the best, since he was unsure he wanted the FBI and governments to have those ships until they weren't so inclined for wars.

Once Lois was out of the hospital, she and Mel went back to the Ormond Garage to talk to Doc and Nani. That's when Mel found out Nani had disappeared without a trace. Doc and Mel drove out to where the ship had crashed, and it was gone. Mel guessed Nani thought like he did. Humans weren't ready for these ships yet.

8

A NEW FUTURE

After the accident, Mel quit the FBI, and he and Lois ran their insurance agency until Mel's untimely death in 1984. Lois never regained the memory of the ship, Nani the Sasquatch, or any of her adventures on the ship, but she always retained her love and attraction for Ormond Beach Florida. When Mel passed away, Lois moved to Florida, and into the Bear Creek Senior Community, but then that's another story.

ABOUT THE AUTHOR

Patrick Talmadge Sr. has always been a late bloomer. His growth didn't cease until he was over 21 years old. He reached his pinnacle as a national and world-class masters middle-distance runner at the age of 37, when he won his first master's national track and field championship in the 800-meter run.

At 47, Patrick earned his Bachelor of Arts degree and made history as the oldest NCAA cross-country runner. Seven years later, at 54, he returned to college to pursue a Master's degree in Psychology. During this time, he ran the mile in track, once again setting a record as the oldest NCAA track and field runner. He received his Master's degree in Psychology at 57. At the age of 66, he embarked on his writing journey.

Patrick taught himself to read at the tender age of three and a half and has been an avid reader ever since. With a keen interest in all fields of science, science fiction, and fantasy, he amassed a wealth of knowledge that would later prove invaluable when he began writing. Throughout his 20s and 30s, Patrick devoured two to three books a day. Upon graduating from graduate school in 2011, he retired from competitive running and felt a growing desire to write the stories that had been simmering within him.

In November 2021, spurred on by the love of his life, Patrick began his writing career. By July 2023, he had completed an adult four-book science fiction series about Sasquatch, a four-book children's series on the same subject, and a standalone novel about a senior community that befriends a troupe of Sasquatch.

Patrick possesses a unique ability to write multiple stories simultaneously, allowing him to modify and adjust interconnected narratives for clarity when writing a series. With a bit of luck, Patrick will continue to pursue his passion for writing for the rest of his life, or at least until his computer gives out.

ALSO BY PATRICK TALMADGE

Hidden Mountain Chronicles

Sasquatch Race

Sasquatch Prison Diary

Tenino Caverns

Sasquatch Home Planet

Sasquatch Chronicles

Hunter and Noah vs. Sasquatch Vol. 1

Hunter and Noah vs. Sasquatch Vol. 2

Hunter and Noah vs. Sasquatch Vol. 3

Hunter and Noah vs. Sasquatch Vol. 4

Sasquatch Senior Community Series

Sasquatch Senior Community

Sasquatch Senior Community: Lois and Mel the Beginning

Sasquatch Senior Community: The Early Years

Sasquatch Senior Community: The Middle Years

AFTERWORD

Go to hangar1publishing.com to learn more about the Authors and stay up to date with their newest releases.

www.ingramcontent.com/pod-product-compliance
Lightning Source LLC
Chambersburg PA
CBHW071545120626
46550CB00006B/2586